Smelly, Stinky Skunk

TEACHING ADJECTIVES

BY YVONNE PEARSON

The Child's World®
childsworld.com

Published by The Child's World®
1980 Lookout Drive • Mankato, MN 56003-1705
800-599-READ • www.childsworld.com

ACKNOWLEDGMENTS
The Child's World®: Mary Swensen, Publishing Director
Red Line Editorial: Editorial direction and production
The Design Lab: Design

Photographs ©: Eric Isselee/Shutterstock Images, cover, 1, 2-3, 5;
Shutterstock Images, 4, 10; Peter Kirillov/Shutterstock Images, 6-7;
Natalya Rozhkova/Shutterstock Images, 8-9; Volodymyr Burdiak/
Shutterstock Images, 11; Bridget Calip/Shutterstock Images, 12;
Margo Harrison/Shutterstock Images, 14-15

ISBN 9781503808423
LCCN 2015958429

Printed in the United States of America
Mankato, MN
June, 2016
PAO2304

ABOUT THE AUTHOR
Yvonne Pearson is a poet who loves to play
with words. She also writes essays and books.
She lives in Minneapolis, Minnesota.

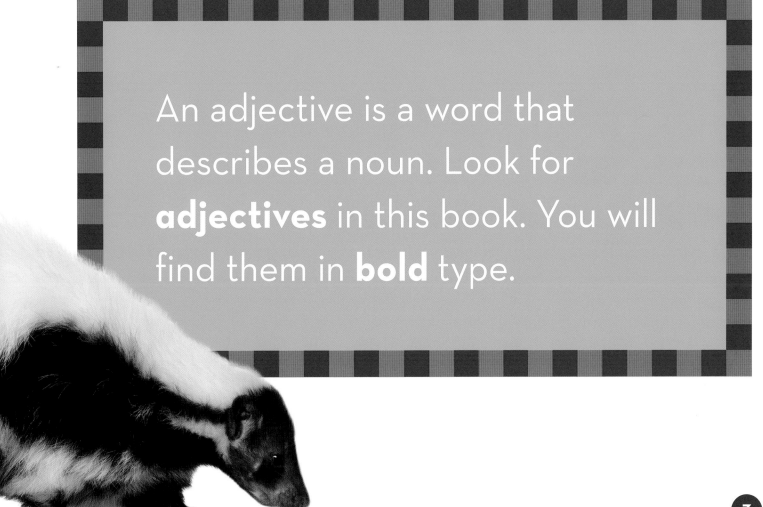

An adjective is a word that describes a noun. Look for **adjectives** in this book. You will find them in **bold** type.

A skunk sprays a **bad** smell to keep **other** animals away. Stay away from a **smelly**, **stinky** skunk!

The **funny** puppy chases his **red** ball. He falls splat on the **hard** floor. The **little** puppy gets right back up to play.

Zebras have **black** and **white** stripes. **Each zebra's** stripes are **different** from the stripes of all **other** zebras.

The **happy** giraffe has a **long** neck. It eats **tender green** leaves from **tall** trees.

The **big brown** bear eats **ripe** berries. The **bright** sun warms its **thick** fur.

A **cranky** horse throws the **large** cowboy from its back. The cowboy is **glad** he did not get hurt.

Did you find these adjectives?

bad	large
big	little
black	long
bright	other
brown	red
cranky	ripe
different	smelly
each	stinky
funny	tall
glad	tender
green	thick
happy	white
hard	zebra's

To Learn More

IN THE LIBRARY

Dolinskiy, Irina Gonikberg. *Parts of Speech Parade*. Longwood, FL: Mark Wayne Adams, 2015.

First Grade Big Workbook. Grand Haven, MI: School Zone, 2015.

Language Arts. Greensboro, NC: Spectrum, 2011.

ON THE WEB

Visit our Web site for links about adjectives: **childsworld.com/links**

Note to Parents, Teachers, and Librarians: We routinely verify our Web links to make sure they are safe and active sites. So encourage your readers to check them out!